Serial Killers: Top 15 Most Evil Serial Killers To Ever Live And The True Stories Of Their Crimes

TABLE OF CONTENTS

INTRODUCTION

Ted Bundy

John Wayne Gacy Jr

The Zodiac Killer

Jeffery Dahmer

Gary Ridgway

Richard Ramirez

H. H. Holmes

Denis Rader

David Berkowitz

Edmund Kemper

Aileen Wuornos

Ed Gein

Leonard Lake & Charles Ng

Boston Strangler

Angelo Buono, Jr.

CONCLUSION

INTRODUCTION

Thanks in no small part to the billion dollar movie industries in different parts of the world that release tonnes of serial-killer-themed movies on a yearly basis and writers and authors who publish thousands of novels and story books that portray the lives of fictional serial killers; we have become accustomed to the phrase "serial killers". A common idiom says that "familiarity breeds contempt"; this idiom is largely true and it is fact reflected in the way we associate criminals with the phrase "serial killers". It is not uncommon to see a toddler or perhaps, even a teenager who has spent hours watching a movie series centered around the life of a serial killer begin to associate just about every criminal activity he hears on the news with serial killing. Consequently, statements like "Dad, I heard the FBI finally apprehended the man who fatally shot aunt Serena at the park… the man must be a serial killer." The reasons for this apparent common misinterpretation of serial killing or perhaps more appropriately, serial killer is not exactly farfetched.

Just as there seems to be a form of chaos regarding the use of the phrase "serial killer", there also seem to be a form of "disorderliness" regarding the origin of serial killer; even though it must be said that there appears to be a consensus in the case of the latter, especially of recent. It is widely believed that the phrase was first used in an English Language book titled *The Complete Detective*; the book written by Richard Hughes was published in 1950. However, recent research credits the first use of the phrase albeit in German to Ernst August Ferdinand Gennat, the Director of the Berlin Criminal Police, around 20 years before *The Complete Detective* was published (1931 to be precise). In the new age however, FBI Special Agent, Robert Ressler, who was one of the founding members of the Bureau's elite Behavioral Science Unit receives a larger chunk of the recognition for inventing the phrase "serial killer". According to Robert Ressler, he fell in love with the phrase when the FBI where attempting to solve the case of the notorious serial killer "Son of Sam" (who coincidentally we are going to look at) in the 1970s. Before we begin to explore the lives of Son of Sam and other infamous serial killers this country has ever had I think it's only fair that we fully comprehend what makes an individual a serial killer. Just like other knock-on themes surrounding serial killer(s), the definition of what constitutes of a serial killer still generates debate even up until today. The main area of the definition of serial killer which springs up debate is the number of murder victims a serial killer should have. While the FBI puts it as a series of two or more murders committed by an individual other experts like psychologists and related professionals are of the opinion that the murder victims of serial killer should be a minimum of three. Despite this difference in the number of murder victims of a serial killer, the consensus is that uncharacteristic psychological satisfaction, financial rewards, physical and sexual delight, and aberrant search for ecstasy are often times the deciding factor in the heinous behavior of serial killers. Another critical part of serial killing is that the murder events must have taken place at different times; this break between events is often called the "cooling off period". Despite the apparent disparity in the "numerical victim-composition" of a serial killer, one thing is certain: they largely murder people at unprecedented rate and nobody wants to be friends with a serial killer, well, except he or she is also a serial killer or a related criminal.

That's that about that about the origin, definition, debate and whatnots about a serial killer. You certainly did not pick this text because you are interested in the coining of the phrase "serial killers" or its definition (even though it might interest you); your inclination towards this material is largely because you are interested in knowing about the true stories of 15 of the most evil serial killers to ever grace the surface of the earth. Flip to the next page to begin your adventurous ride!

Ted Bundy

Just as the sun was setting down on the eastern shore of Lake Champlain, few miles away from the hustle and bustle of Burlington, Vermont, USA, a baby boy was born to Eleanor Louise Cowell, a single mother on November 24, 1946. That baby was named Theodore Robert Cowell (Later, Theodore Robert Bundy). And unlike the aura of innocence, naivety and bliss that enveloped his birth at the Elizabeth Lund Home for Unwed Mothers in Vermont, he grew up to be a creator of sadness, sorrow and thorough anguish. He was to create this aura by being a serial killer, rapist, necrophile and a kidnapper. And more often than not, his victims were the opposite sex. Bundy suffered his fair share of ignominy as a child, especially because it was rumored that his grandfather might have been his biological father thus making him a product of incest. Ted Bundy grew up to be a young man who prided himself on his good looks; and according to him it was his apparent charm and his handsomeness he leveraged upon to lure young women eventually making them murder victims. He embarked on killing spree that lasted for about five years and in at least seven states across America; from 1974 to 1979. And it is only five years because his first documented crime was in 1974. Although according to unverified reports, he also committed murder amongst other crimes from his teenage years. In fact, incidental evidence suggests that he committed his murder when he was 14; and an 8-year-old Ann Marie Burr was the victim. It should however be noted that he denied this crime as he did so many other crimes that he allegedly committed. As a proof of his superficial penchant for lies and deceit, he told several crime detectives and psychologists different details about the crimes he committed. He implicitly told homicide detective Robert Keppel that he killed someone in Seattle in 1972 and another person in Washington in 1973. To establish his profile as arguably the most prolific serial killer in the history of the US he confessed to the atrocious murders of at least 36 women; this is despite the notion among authorities that his victims were closer to 100 in number. His first documented victim was 18 year-old Karen Sparks, a student at UW; he used a metal rod from her bed frame to beat her numerous times, he then subsequently assaulted her with a dioptra. She eventually suffered a permanent brain damage despite the best efforts of medical professionals. Bundy's record with females was so prolific that female college students disappeared so frequently and often times, the missing students were all later found to be murdered and severely mutilated. He was executed by electrocution in 1989 after confessing to several crimes. He eliminated any iota of innocence (if there was indeed any) people had about him by attempting to use a victim to remain alive on the electric chair. As is the case with most fascinating and "heroic" serial killers, a movie adaptation of the life and crimes of Ted Bundy was released in 2002. The movie which starred Michael Burke as the lead actor gave us a visual insight into the lifestyle of the iniquitous Ted Bundy.

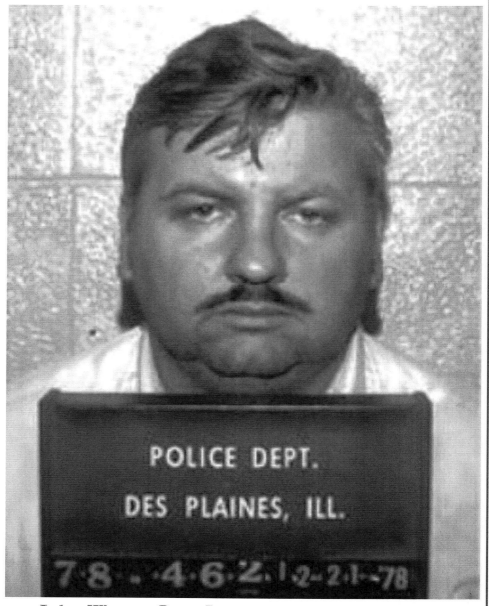

John Wayne Gacy Jr

Most sociologists, psychologists and other professionals who are experts in the field of human behavior are of the opinion that the upbringing, childhood period of any individual are more often than not the formative factor about the overall behavior of such an individual when he or she becomes a fully fledged adult. John Wayne Gacy epitomized this assertion. John Wayne Gacy Junior was born into a middle-class, Irish catholic family, on March 1942. He was the second son of three children born to an auto repair machinist veteran father and a homemaker mother. He was a constant victim of physical abuse by his father who extolled behaviors such as being highly volatile, alcoholic and homophobia. As an example of his father's violent nature, it was reported that a young Gacy at 7 years-old was beaten by his father with a razor strop after his father was informed Gacy and his friend were caught sexually fondling a young girl. Fast forward to 1964, Gacy got married for the first time to co-worker Marlynn Myers; he had two children from that marriage. After accusations of molestation at his workplace, he was sentenced to ten years in prison for sodomy thus his wife divorced him. However, he was released after a year and six months because of his good behavior in the facility.

He later married Carole Hofgren, a divorcee with two daughters. To further prove the improvement in his character, he often dressed up as a clown to entertain sick children and at random children parties. Consequently, his nickname "Killer Clown" was fashioned. Gacy was indeed a serial killer in every sense of that phrase "serial killer". His convictions included: 1 count of sodomy, 33 counts of murder, 1 count of sexual assault, and 1 count of indecent liberties with a child. His first recorded murder victim was 16-year-old Timothy Jack McCoy just after New Year's Day in 1972. After murdering the young Timothy McCoy by stabbing him multiple times with a kitchen knife, Gacy buried McCoy in his crawl space and subsequently covered his remains with concrete to conceal his terrible actions. Two years later, Gacy also confirmed killing an unnamed teenager in his room by strangling him. Rather startlingly, he buried the teenager about 15 feet from the barbecue pit in his backyard. Before injecting him with lethal injection, 52-year-old mustered this final words "Kiss my ass." He was indeed an unrepentant serial killer!

The Zodiac Killer

The Zodiac Killer is perhaps the most unique serial killer to grace the surface of the US because he remained anonymous throughout his existence or perhaps even non-existence. In similar fashion, his date of birth, date of death and even his cause of death have not been established up till this day. Nevertheless, his span and location of his operations are not in oblivion to authorities, as it is recorded that he murdered victims in Lake Berryessa, San Fransisco, Benicia and Valleji between December 1968 and October 1969. Most of his victims were newly married couples or male and female partners who dwelled in isolated areas. He was also known to be apt at using both guns and knives to commit his atrocities. It is believed that his first murder victims were high school students David Faraday and Betty Lou Jensen. He reportedly murdered them while they were planning to attend Christmas concert which was coincidentally their first date; it is understood that he killed both victims with a gun. The Zodiac, as he was often called murdered quite a number of people in the late 1960s and early 1970s. As a practice of his, he would often write letters which largely contain physical evidence from his crime to local newspapers and demand that his letters were published. He frequently sent cryptograms which he claimed enclosed his identity; this was obviously to cause more panic among people. In one of his letters he claimed he killed 37 people even though authorities put this figure at 7 though the same authorities agree that could be more than 7 but the other victims are merely suspected victims. There were recent investigations into the identity of the Zodiac by the San Francisco police department however they recently halted their investigations.

Jeffery Dahmer

On May 21, 1960, an American serial killer and serial sex offender by the name of Jeffrey Dahmer was born in Milwaukee, Wisconsin to Lionel Herbert and Joyce Dahmer. However, according to those who were quite familiar with his childhood especially before he became a teenager, there was no reason to suggest that he would tread that path in his later years. He was reported to be a child who was bubbly and happy in his early childhood years. Things began to change as his parents became to pay him less attention; this was largely due to his mother's attention-seeking nature and his father's constant absence from home which was due to his tertiary education at the university. A particular thing of interest about Dahmer's early years was his allure towards dead animals. This reportedly sprung up at an early age when he saw his father removing animal bones from under their house. Between the ages of 10 and 15, he began to really express his weird passion towards dead animals by dismembering their bones; he usually did this with a large volumes of alcohol thus he became an alcoholic. Fast forward to the summer of 1978, 18-years-old Jeffery Dahmer committed his first murder. His victim was a hitchhiker by the name of Steven Hicks who offered to take Dahmer to his father's house to drink beer. There was a bizarre turn of events at Dahmer's house when all of a sudden Dahmer decided to hit Hicks with a 10 lb dumbbell at the rear of his head; Dahmer subsequently confessed that he killed Hicks because he didn't want to leave the house. He buried Hick's body in his backyard. Between 1987 and 1989 he killed at least two more people. Most times, he would pick up his victims from bars and restaurants; he would subsequently have sex with them (gays) and then kill them. By the summer of 1991, his killings had become more frequent at the rate of one per week. He had a bizarre premonition that his victims could become "zombies" to be used as consensual sexual partners. Dahmer was indicted on 17 murder charges, he however pleaded not guilty despite the vast evidence against him. He based his not guilty plea on insanity. He was finally sentenced to a total of 957 years in prison for his numerous atrocities. Dahmer prison term was however cut short as he was fatally injured by a fellow prison inmate in November of 1994. Only last year, his killer, Christopher Scarver, said he grew to despise Dahmer because he would fashion severed limbs out of prison food to taunt other inmates.

Gary Ridgway

Gary Ridgway (aka The Green River Killer) was the born as the second of the three children in Salt Lake City, Utah in 1949. He had a very turbulent childhood, and was particularly poor in his performance in school. It was also reported that he had an IQ of 82 which is below the mark for average intelligence. He was rightly dubbed the most prolific American serial killer in history as the number of confirmed murder convictions stand at 49 even though he professes that he has murdered more than 80 people mostly women. His method of killing his victims which were mostly women in underprivileged positions such as prostitutes, and naïve teenage girls was by strangulation even though there are evidences that he murdered some with the aid of ligatures. Inexplicably, he would later have sex with the dead bodies which he would long dumped in forested areas of King County. Ridgway had a decent early life; he graduated from Tyee High School in 1969 and married in the same year. Things turned for the worse when started having regular sexual escapades with prostitutes while in the Navy. This led to dissolution of his marriage. According to his numerous exes, Ridgway was sexually violent and he was simply never satisfied. His penchant for using ligatures instead of his hand to strangle his victims was because of the marks and bruises his victims left on his hand most times. In late 2003, Ridgway entered a guilty plea to 48 charges of aggravated first degree murder as part of a plea bargain that would spare him execution for his cooperation in locating the remains of his victims and related details. In his words 'I want to prove there's 80 bodies out there'. The search for some of the missing bodies is still on till today.

Richard Ramirez

"I love to kill people. I love watching them die. I would shoot them in the head and they would wiggle and squirm all over the place, and then just stop. Or I would cut them with a knife and watch their faces turn real white. I love all that blood. I told one lady to give me all her money. She said no. So I cut her and pulled her eyes out." This is one the most remarkable quotes of serial killer and rapist, Richard Ramirez, aka The Night Crawler. It shows just how vicious the man was. Ramirez was given birth to in El Paso, Texas on February 29, 1960. He was the last of five children. As is the case with other infamous serial killers, Ramirez had a rather isolated childhood experience. He realized that he had epilepsy in his fifth grade; doctors informed him that he would eventually outgrow it. The effect of this was his removal from the quarterback position on the football team of his school. By age 10, he started behaving rather weirdly, the high point of his weird actions were the countless nights he spent at cemeteries at his indulgence in smoking marijuana. His cousin, Miguel was a major influence of his derisive lifestyle. In one occasion, he saw Miguel kill his wife with a gun; this reportedly affected a lot of his behaviors and deeds which followed Miguel's murder of his wife. Such deeds included random stealing, petty thieving, burglarizing and abuse of drugs. Another life pattern which followed was an uncanny love and interest in horror movies and Satan. Ramirez moved to Los Angeles after his eighteenth birthday. By this time, he was already an addict of cocaine and was a serial criminal; he interest in Satan also grew extraordinarily, this culminated in him joining the Church of Satan. Several accounts suggested that Ramirez killed his victims mostly at night hence the nickname "Night Crawler"; witnesses said that he often camouflaged in black dresses at night to perpetuate his hideous acts. Certain times, he left satanic pentagrams on his rape victims as a form of autograph. He was sentenced to death of November 7, 1989 and died in prison on June 7, 2013.

H. H. Holmes

Dr. H. H. Holmes (born Herman Webster Mudgett) is widely acclaimed to be the first or at least one of the first set of notorious serial killer to come out of America. He was born on May 16, 1861 in Gilmanton, New Hampshire. Like other serial killers. Holmes was fascinated with putting animals under severe pain while he was a child. His proclivity towards crimes showed its ugly face while he was in college education which he had at University of Michigan; where he successfully graduated to become a medical doctor; he reportedly self-financed his education by effectively duping people through schemes of insurance cons. This was done with a ridiculous trick —he allegedly made requests for "created" people who didn't actually exist and subsequently presented the corpses as the insured. Holmes purchased a store from Elizabeth Holton at the northwest corner of South Wallace Avenue in the Englewood neighborhood; the empty lot across the drugstore which he purchased was nicknamed "the castle" because of its massive structure and size. The store was used as a hostelry for the World's Columbian Exposition in 1893. While constructing the castle (World's Fair Hotel), Holmes established an informal relationship with Benjamin Pitezel who became his partner in crime. On completion of the hotel, Holmes reportedly abused his female employees sexually. Some of his victims which he had a psychological and financial 'grip' suffered various forms of death. It was reported that he killed some victims by hanging them in the "secret hanging chamber" which was located on the second floor; some other victims died by suffocation while a few died of malnutrition and hunger. Holmes was finally arrested after evading authorities by moving across several states in St. Louis. However, he was bailed out. While in prison he conjured a plan with another prison inmate which involved scamming an unsuspecting lawyer via his insurance wiles. In October of 1895, Holmes was put on trial for killing Benjamin Pitezel, he was then sentenced to death. By then, it was clear that he was also responsible for Pitezel's children whom up until that point were missing. He was hanged on May 7, 1986 in Philadelphia County Prison.

Denis Rader

Denis Rader was also known as the BTK killer; BTK meaning blind, torture and kill. He has been characterized as a sadist-fetishist by murder experts. Rader was born on March 9, 1945 in a relatively serene part of Kansas. He was the first of four sons born to William and Dorothea Rader. Rader had quiet upbringing as there was nothing to suggest he would one day grow up to become an astute serial killer, especially as he was actively involved in church activities from a tender age.

However, his tendencies to be all by himself most times made him to start having thoughts that were outright wicked and evil. He reportedly began to daydream about torturing young girls and abusing them intensely. By the time he became a young man, he purportedly began killing pets. In fact, he later admitted that he killed dogs and cats in his youthful age. After graduating from Wichita Heights High School in 1963, he found a job in a grocery store. In a bid to avoid joining the Vietnam War team he joined the US Air Force. According to him, he spent time in countries like Turkey, Greece, Japan and Korea while in the US Air Force. By then, his thirst for torturing and killing people had increased greatly. He wandered around different parts of the US seeking for "suitable" victims. Unfortunately for the Otero family, he found them perfect for his evil thoughts. On January 15, 1974, he came through the back door of the Otero's residence with a kit which contained a gun, cords, knives and break-in devices; he did this after cutting off the phone line belonging to the family. He murdered the entire family: he used a cord signature to strangle the father, Joe and his 9-year-old son Joey; he killed the 11 year old child in a cruel manner by hanging her from a plumbing pipe before he subsequently masturbated on her legs which were open. He reportedly had about 10 victims spanning 1974 to 1991. He was successfully apprehended by authorities on February 25, 2005; he was formally charged three days later with 10 counts of first degree murder. He was sentenced to life imprisonment with no parole for 175 years on August 18, 2005.

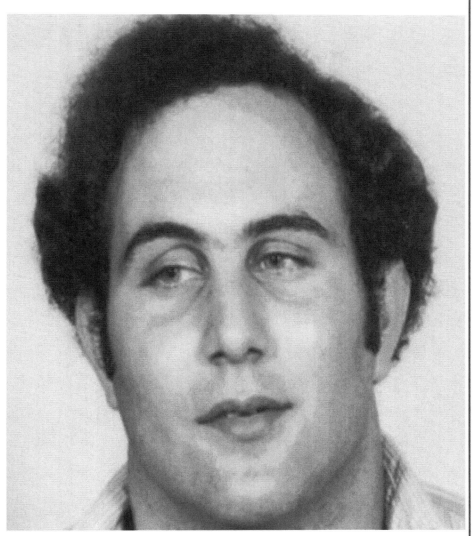

David Berkowitz

In *Murderpedia,* the encyclopedia of murderers, David Richard Berkowitz is characterized with the following words "claimed that neighbor's dog, Harvey, was possessed by an ancient demon and that it issued commands to Berkowitz to kill". David Richard Berkowitz (aka Son of Sam or the .44 Caliber killer) is an

American serial killer who took pride in terrorizing American inhabitants, particularly those who resided in New York City. An infant David was abandoned by his biological mother and was adopted by Pearl and Nathan Berkowitz of the Bronx; who raised the young infant as their only child. It is alleged that Berkowitz had a relatively turbulent childhood; as an indication of his troublesome nature his parents reportedly made consultations with psychotherapists on numerous occasions about the difficult nature of their adopted child. In 1971, eighteen-year-old Berkowitz joined the US Army and thus served in South Korea and in the US. He was discharged three years later amidst much fanfare and admiration. What happened next seemingly changed his life pattern. Berkowitz located his biological matter who divulged details about his illicit birth. He subsequently fell out of contact with his mother as begun his race to survive alone. He had decent official jobs in New York. Berkowitz confessed that he committed his first murder on December 24, 1975 by stabbing two women using a hunting knife; one of the victims remains unidentified till this day. About 6 months he committed his next murder, he strode up to a car containing 18-year-old Donna Lauria and 19-year-old Jody Valenti and shot at them. Valenti survived while Lauria died on the spot. After several witness accounts and police investigations it was realized that a .44 caliber Bulldog gun was use to commit the crime. Berkowitz committed more murders October 23, and November 27 of the same year. He also shot at a car containing Christine Freund and John Diel on January 30, 1977. On April 17, 1977, Berkowitz used the same .44 caliber gun to add two more victims to his growing list of victims. Police discovered a letter Berkowitz addressed to the captain of NYPD in which he referred to himself as the Son of Sam and his intentions to continue his heinous crimes. After confessing to his crimes, Berkowitz was sentenced to six life sentences for his six murder victims.

Edmund Kemper

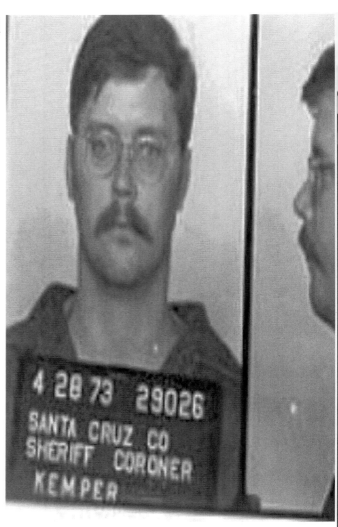

Like other infamous serial killers, Kemper's childhood was saturated with different forms of abuse and turmoil. Edmund Emil Kemper III was born on December 18,

1948; and he's nicknamed The Co-ed Butcher or The Co-ed killer. He reportedly had parents who very violent, especially with their actions and words. Kemper suffered from constant ignominy of tirades of physical abuse and punishments from his unforgiving parents. A typical example of such abuse was when his mother made him kill his pet chicken as a form of punishment and then his father ensured that Kemper consumed the dead chicken. On August 26, 1964, 15-year-old Edmund Kemper committed his first murder; and the victims were family members –his grandmother and grandfather. After a heated argument with his grandmother, he angrily picked up a .22 caliber rifle given to him by his grandfather for hunting and lethally shot his grandmother in her head and back. He also shot his grandmother in the driveway when he returned from grocery shopping. After calling the police by himself to report his crimes, he was handed over to the California Youth Authority who sent him for psychiatric testing. It was revealed that he had paranoid schizophrenia. After serving five years and proving that he was safe to integrate with people he was released to his remarried mother (despite hospital psychiatrists disapproving it). He had a difficult relationship with his mother after their reunion as they fell into constant heated arguments. After becoming financially independent he decided to leave his mother's house to rent an apartment with his friend in Alameda. Fast forward to a few years later, Kemper become more deadly as he embarked on a killing spree that engulfed six female students, his mother and her best friend. His modus operandi involved shooting, stabbing, or smothering his female victims while they were hitchhiking and then performing sexual acts with their corpses before dissecting and dismembering them. He performed the same shocking act on his mother on April 20, 1973. Kemper was indicted on 8 counts of first degree murder on May 7, 1963. He is currently serving a life sentence at

Vacaville, California; and recent reports indicate that he is not interested in leaving the prison.

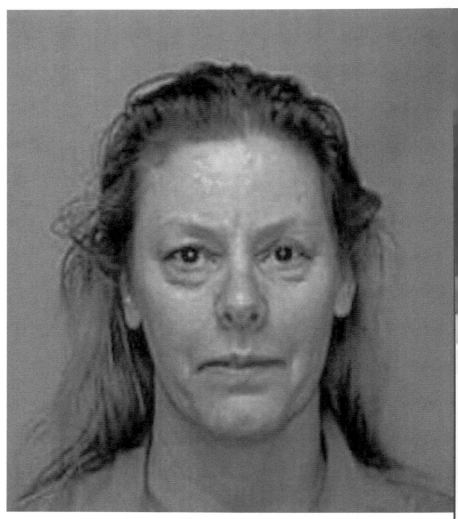

Aileen Wuornos

Like few notorious serial killers who added spices of intrigue in committing their preposterous acts, the life of Aileen Wuornos has remade in a movie title "Monster". The Oscar-winning movie which stars popular actress, Charlize Theron as the lead actor was released in 2003. Alien Wuornos was born Aileen Carol Pittman on February 29, 1956 in Rochester, Michigan, US, to her mother, Diane Wuornos ,who got married at the age of

14 to Leo Dale Pittman. Unfortunately for Wuornos she never got to meet her father as he hung himself in prison after being convicted of several secual crimes against children. Wuornos lived a carefree life right from her early childhood years to her pre-teenage years. She reported began trading by barter, sexual activities for items like food and drugs; she later alleged that these behaviors were borne from constant sexual abuse by her grandfather while she was a little girl. At age 14 she became pregnant as a result of rape by her grandfather's friend. She resorted to prostitution after grandfather threw her out of his house. By the late 1970s, she moved to Florida to continue her prostitution adventure; it was then that her interest in robbery and murder grew alongside prostitution. She did this with an acquaintance of hers-Tyria Moore. Between 1989 and 1990, the men she had murdered were at least 6 who engaged in sexual activities with her. A minor traffic accident in one of her victim's car led to her arrest and eventual 2002 execution.

She died at the age of 46. It is pertinent to note that unlike most serial killers she became famous after her death.

Ed Gein

Ed Gein, aka The Mad Butcher or the "real" American psycho was a serial killer who had an inclination towards body snatching. He was born on August 27, 1906 in La Crosse County, Wisconsin and died on July 26, 1984 in

Madison, Wisconsin due to heart and respiratory failure. It was reported that he was a loner while growing up in the tiny farming community in Wisconsin. He lived around the farming area with his overbearing brother who over and over again told him that sex was very aberrant. Their farmhouse turned to a "mad man's cave" when his authoritarian mother died in 1945 after his brother died a year earlier. The degeneration into a mad man's place was largely because Ed Gein had become so emotionally attached his domineering family relations. He stayed alone in the large house; nonetheless he made the house "smaller" by locking at least six rooms which included his late mother's room (who he claimed her ghost mocked him). He suddenly develop weird fantasies which included interest in the massacres committed by the Nazis during World War II, literature on female anatomy, horror novels and porn magazines. His interest grew into physical acts when he began excavating decayed female corpses in Wisconsin cemeteries at night. He ostensibly derived satisfaction by taking pieces of dead parts of the bodies (especially sexual organs) to create a sort of cloth over his body which he wore while dancing round the homestead. After a while, he began to seek fresher corpses to cure his uncontrollable thirst for female corpses. His victims were mostly women above the age of 50. Strewn remains of about fifteen bodies which were most likely feminine were found at his house. He was adjudged to be fit for trial after spending ten years in a mental facility. On July 26, 1984, Gein died of respiratory failure due to long cancer at the age of 77 in Mendota Mental Health Institute. His story is very popular thus it has appeared in series of magazine, literature, movies and music.

Leonard Lake & Charles Ng

Leonard Lake and Charles Ng were an effective pair of serial killers, robbers and rapists. They reportedly committed about 25 murders between 1983 and 1985. Lake was born in San Francisco, California on October 29, 1945 while Ng was born to wealthy Chinese family in Hong Kong on December 24, 1960. Lake was fixated with pornography while growing up even though he was pretty brilliant. Ng on the other hand was a troubled loner while growing up in Singapore. He eventually moved to the US on a student visa in 1978 to study biology at the College of Notre Dame in Belmont California; this was after committing several petty crimes in Singapore and England. His paths crossed with that of Leonard Lake after dropping out of college after just a semester. He enlisted in the United States Marine Corps to evade persecution for a hit-and-run accident he was involved in. He was dishonorably discharged from the Marine Corps after his involvement in theft of heavy weaponry. Lake and Ng were notorious for making women their victims. However their target for women meant that the entire family of such women could become victims if they were caught in operation. It is reported that they would firstly make children and men their first murder victims to ensure they could be "free" to do whatever they wanted to do with their female victims. They raped, tortured and eventually killed the victims; they often performed these acts while the other person was videotaping the acts. After which they often dismembered and buried their victims in shallow graves. Ng was apprehended on July 6, 1985, and is facing a death penalty till today while Lake committed suicide by taking cyanide pills.

Boston Strangler

The Boston Strangler was an unidentified serial killer who murdered a minimum of 13(other reports put the figure at 11) women via between 1962 and 1964 strangulation accompanied by some form of sexual assault. Despite the supposed assertion that the Boston Strangler was unidentified, the crimes were however linked to Alberto DeSalvo based on his confession and DNA evidence connecting him to the last murder victim. However, crime experts still express serious doubts regarding the validity of the confession of Alberto DeSalvo. The Boston Strangler terrorized Boston, particularly women living alone. Often times, his victims were found with their own nylons wrapped several times around their necks and tied with a bow. The frequency of the murders was fortnightly though there were certain periods were there was no case of murder. It was deduced that the Boston Strangler must have established a sort of close relationship with his victims as there was hardly a case of him forcing himself through any of the victims' homes. Conversely, it could also mean that he was tact at breaking-in to his victims' homes. In October of 1964, a young woman reported a man claiming to be a detective tied her to bed and began to rape her; and then suddenly apologized and left, her description of the man aided police in deciphering that DeSalvo was the culprit.

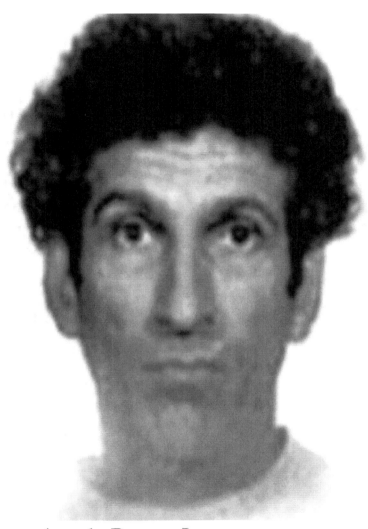

Angelo Buono, Jr.

Angelo Buono, Jr. was born Angelo Anthony Buono, Jr, in Rochester, NY to Italian-American emigrants from San Buono, Italy. His parents divorced while he was a toddler thus he moved to stay with his mother and sister in Glendale, California. He was reportedly very sexual at a tender age. He claimed to have assaulted several girls while he was a teenager. He also reportedly worshipped and adored serial rapist Caryl Chessman from a tender age. He married his high-school sweetheart, 17-year-old Geraldine Vinal whom he impregnated. He left her after a week. In 1975, Buono ran into his cousin Kenneth Bianchi; together they became the infamous Hillside Stranglers due to the numerous victims they killed by strangulation. Buono and Bianchi began prostituting women after they met. Their trick apparently involved driving around Los Angeles in Buono's car with fake police badges which they used to convince women that they were undercover policemen. Once they are successful in compelling the women into their cars, they would then drive them to Buono's house where they were sexually assaulted, tortured and finally murdered. Their victims ranged from age 14 to 28. It is worth mentioning that they also used techniques such as carbon monoxide poisoning and electrocution to kill some of their victims. In 1986, Buono married Christine Kizuka. Bianchi informed Buono that he was being questioned about the Hillside Stranglers. The case against Buono was based on the confessions of his partner, Bianchi. The jury eventually convicted Buono on nine counts of murder, assault, rape, and failure to pay child support after his trial lasted for two years-from November 1981 to November 1983. Buono died of a heart attack in his cell. He was aged 67.

CONCLUSION

There you have it, a brief exposition on the exploits of 15 serial killers to grace the surface of the earth. You should be rest assured that your curiosity about the lives of serial killers is nothing new rather it is something that is pretty insidious in our modern day lives; thanks to our no-holds-barred access to TV shows, movies, novels, comics and even theatre plays, amongst others. Moreover, a few of us might have had friends, relations, distant relations, acquaintances or even foes that have fallen prey to the dastardly deeds of serial killers, thus it is only fair that our inquisitive nature has driven us to try to understand the inner workings of the lifestyle of serial killers. Even if this is not your case, your quest for knowledge especially one that is informative and can be improbably exhilarating should only be applauded by all and sundry. On a final note, James Hoare, editor of Real Crime, a monthly magazine that was launched in the UK on August 2015 responded to the question of why people find serial killers so enthralling by saying that "They represent something larger than life, something truly cartoonishly monstrous, like the horror stories you're told as a child". Isn't this something worth exploring?